JAMES, PETER, AND JUDE

THE CATHOLIC LETTERS

Clifford M. Yeary

"Catholic Letters" refers to seven New Testament letters (James; 1 and 2 Peter; 1, 2, and 3 John; and Jude). They were thought to have had a more universal audience than the Pauline letters, thus the designation "catholic."

This Study Guide focuses on those catholic letters found in the New Collegeville Bible Commentary by Patrick J. Hartin: *James, First Peter, Jude, Second Peter*.

The Little Rock Scripture Study that includes 1, 2, and 3 John is called *The Gospel According to John and the Johannine Letters*.

LITTLE ROCK SCRIPTURE STUDY

A ministry of the Diocese of Little Rock
in partnership with Liturgical Press

DIOCESE OF LITTLE ROCK

2500 North Tyler Street • P.O. Box 7565 • Little Rock, Arkansas 72217 • (501) 664-0340 Fax (501) 664-6304

Dear Friends in Christ,

Sacred Scripture is a wealth of inspired wisdom expressing Christian truths which challenge us to deepen our relationship with God. Although the Bible can be intimidating, it is important that we study God's word in the Scriptures, because it is the basis of our faith and offers us the thoughts and experiences of Christians past and present. It is God speaking to us through the insights of Church fathers and later saints.

I am pleased to present this study guide from Little Rock Scripture Study to serve as an aid for reflection and contemplation in your reading of Scripture. At the same time, the guide will give you insight into how to apply what you have read to your life today.

I encourage you to read Sacred Scripture slowly and reflectively so that it can penetrate your heart and mind. It is my hope that the Word of God will empower you as Christians to live a life worthy of your call as a child of God and a member of the body of Christ.

Sincerely in Christ,

✝ Anthony B. Taylor
Bishop of Little Rock

Sacred Scripture

"The Church has always venerated the divine Scriptures just as she venerates the body of the Lord, since from the table of both the word of God and of the body of Christ she unceasingly receives and offers to the faithful the bread of life, especially in the sacred liturgy. She has always regarded the Scriptures together with sacred tradition as the supreme rule of faith, and will ever do so. For, inspired by God and committed once and for all to writing, they impart the word of God Himself without change, and make the voice of the Holy Spirit resound in the words of the prophets and apostles. Therefore, like the Christian religion itself, all the preaching of the Church must be nourished and ruled by sacred Scripture. For in the sacred books, the Father who is in heaven meets His children with great love and speaks with them; and the force and power in the word of God is so great that it remains the support and energy of the Church, the strength of faith for her sons, the food of the soul, the pure and perennial source of spiritual life."

Vatican II, Dogmatic Constitution on Divine Revelation, no. 21.

INTERPRETATION OF SACRED SCRIPTURE

"Since God speaks in sacred Scripture through men in human fashion, the interpreter of sacred Scripture, in order to see clearly what God wanted to communicate to us, should carefully investigate what meaning the sacred writers really intended, and what God wanted to manifest by means of their words.

"Those who search out the intention of the sacred writers must, among other things, have regard for 'literary forms.' For truth is proposed and expressed in a variety of ways, depending on whether a text is history of one kind or another, or whether its form is that of prophecy, poetry, or some other type of speech. The interpreter must investigate what meaning the sacred writer intended to express and actually expressed in particular circumstances as he used contemporary literary forms in accordance with the situation

3

of his own time and culture. For the correct understanding of what the sacred author wanted to assert, due attention must be paid to the customary and characteristic styles of perceiving, speaking, and narrating which prevailed at the time of the sacred writer, and to the customs men normally followed in that period in their everyday dealings with one another."

Vatican II, Dogmatic Constitution on Divine Revelation, no. 12.

Instructions

MATERIALS FOR THE STUDY

This Study Guide: James, Peter, and Jude: The Catholic Letters

Bible: The New American Bible with Revised New Testament or The New Jerusalem Bible is recommended. Paraphrased editions are discouraged as they offer little if any help when facing difficult textual questions. Choose a Bible you feel free to write in or underline.

Commentary: The New Collegeville Bible Commentary, volume 10, *James, First Peter, Jude, Second Peter* by Patrick J. Hartin (Liturgical Press) is used with this study. The abbreviation for this commentary, NCBC-NT volume 10, and the assigned pages are found at the beginning of each lesson.

ADDITIONAL MATERIALS

Bible Dictionary: *The Dictionary of the Bible* by John L. McKenzie (Simon & Schuster) is highly recommended as a reference.

Notebook: A notebook may be used for lecture notes and your personal reflections.

WEEKLY LESSONS

Lesson 1—James 1–2
Lesson 2—James 3–5

Lesson 3—First Peter 1:1–3:7
Lesson 4—First Peter 3:8–5:14
Lesson 5—Second Peter 1:1–2:16; Jude vv. 1-13
Lesson 6—Second Peter 2:17–3:18; Jude vv. 14-24

YOUR DAILY PERSONAL STUDY

The first step is prayer. Open your heart and mind to God. Reading Scripture is an opportunity to listen to God who loves you. Pray that the same Holy Spirit who guided the formation of Scripture will inspire you to correctly understand what you read and empower you to make what you read a part of your life.

The next step is commitment. Daily spiritual food is as necessary as food for the body. This study is divided into daily units. Schedule a regular time and place for your study, as free from distractions as possible. Allow about twenty minutes a day. Make it a daily appointment with God.

As you begin each lesson read the assigned chapters of Scripture found at the beginning of each lesson, the footnotes in your Bible, and then the indicated pages of the commentary. This preparation will give you an overview of the entire lesson and help you to appreciate the context of individual passages.

As you reflect on Scripture, ask yourself these four questions:

1. *What does the Scripture passage say?*
   Read the passage slowly and reflectively. Use your imagination to picture the scene or enter into it.

2. *What does the Scripture passage mean?*
   Read the footnotes and the commentary to help you understand what the sacred writers intended and what God wanted to communicate by means of their words.

3. *What does the Scripture passage mean to me?*
   Meditate on the passage. God's Word is living and powerful. What is God saying to you today? How does the Scripture passage apply to your life today?

4. *What am I going to do about it?*
    Try to discover how God may be challenging you in this
    passage. An encounter with God contains a challenge to
    know God's will and follow it more closely in daily life.

THE QUESTIONS ASSIGNED FOR EACH DAY

Read the questions and references for each day. The questions
are designed to help you listen to God's Word and to prepare
you for the weekly small-group discussion.

Some of the questions can be answered briefly and objec-
tively by referring to the Bible references and the commentary
(What does the passage say?). Some will lead you to a better
understanding of how the Scriptures apply to the Church,
sacraments, and society *(What does the passage mean?)*. Some
questions will invite you to consider how God's Word chal-
lenges or supports you in your relationships with God and
others *(What does the passage mean to me?)*. Finally, the questions will lead you to examine your actions in light of Scripture
(What am I going to do about it?).

Write your responses in this study guide or in a notebook to
help you clarify and organize your thoughts and feelings.

THE WEEKLY SMALL-GROUP MEETING

The weekly small-group sharing is the heart of the Little Rock
Scripture Study Program. Participants gather in small groups
to share the results of praying, reading, and reflecting on Scripture and on the assigned questions. The goal of the discussion
is for group members to be strengthened and nourished indi-
vidually and as a community through sharing how God's Word
speaks to them and affects their daily lives. The daily study
questions will guide the discussion; it is not necessary to dis-
cuss all the questions.

All members share the responsibility of creating an atmos-
phere of loving support and trust in the group by respecting
the opinions and experiences of others, and by affirming and
encouraging one another. The simple shared prayer which be-
gins and ends each small group meeting also helps create the

open and trusting environment in which group members can share their faith deeply and grow in the study of God's Word.

A distinctive feature of this program is its emphasis on and trust in God's presence working in and through each member. Sharing responses to God's presence in the Word and in others can bring about remarkable growth and transformation.

THE WRAP-UP LECTURE

The lecture is designed to develop and clarify the themes of each lesson. It is not intended to be the focus of the group's discussion. For this reason, the lecture always occurs *after* the small group discussion. If several small groups meet at one time, the groups may gather in a central location to listen to the lecture.

Lectures may be presented by a local speaker. They are also available in audio form on CD and in visual form on DVD.

James 1–2

NCBC-NT VOLUME 10, PAGES 5–20

Day 1

1. Who are the various men named James in the New Testament? (See Mark 1:19; 3:18; Acts 12:2; Gal 1:19.)

2. How does the commentary suggest we should understand the biblical depiction of James as "the brother of the Lord"(Gal 1:19)? (See commentary, pp. 7–8.)

3. What role does Scripture tell us James the brother of the Lord played in the early life of the church? (See Acts 12:17; 15:13-21; 1 Cor 15:7; Jude v. 1.)

Day 2

4. According to the commentary, what is the significance of James being addressed "to the twelve tribes in the dispersion" (1:1)? (See commentary, pp. 8–9.)

5. a) What kinds of situations have taught you the value of perseverance (1:2-3)? (See Luke 8:15; Acts 14:19-22; Heb 12:1-2.)

   b) Can you give examples of unpleasant or difficult circumstances that are not meant to be endured?

6. When have you felt the need for wisdom in making a decision (1:5)?

Day 3

7. What comparison can you draw between James blessing the lowly and warning the rich (1:9-11) and Jesus' statements from his Sermon on the Plain? (See Luke 6:20, 24; also Ps 37:1-2; Isa 40:6-8.)

8. Identify some of the more important gifts you have received from God in your life (1:17).

9. What are some effective ways you can think of to help calm yourself or others when anger or wrath is in danger of flaring up (1:20)?

Day 4

10. If we are to be doers of the Word and not just hearers (1:22), what is the Word asking us to do? (See 1:27; 2:1, 8, 13; Matt 22:38-39.)

11. a) Besides widows and orphans, who else might be especially vulnerable to the effects of poverty in our modern communities (1:27)?

    b) In what ways are our various local religious communities succeeding or failing to demonstrate "pure and undefiled" religion in their regard?

12. In what ways has your faith community worked to meet the challenge to "show no partiality" (2:1-4)? In what ways might it remain a challenge?

Day 5

13. What evidence can you find that God has chosen the poor in the world to be rich in faith (2:5)? (See Matt 5:3; Luke 6:20.)

14. What is the "royal law" (2:8)? (See Lev 19:18b; Matt 22:36-40; Rom 13:9.)

15. How would you explain James's claim that "mercy triumphs over judgment" (2:13)? (See Matt 5:7; 6:14-15; 9:13.)

Day 6

16. How does what James says about faith and works compare with what Paul says about faith and works (2:14-26)? (See Rom 3:28; 4:1-5; Gal 2:15-16; Phil 2:12-13.)

17. Recount the story of Abraham and the sacrifice of Isaac (2:21-23). (See Gen 22:1-18.)

18. What is the story of Rahab the harlot (2:25)? (See Josh 2:1-24; 6:16-25; Matt 1:5.)

James 3–5

NCBC-NT VOLUME 10, PAGES 20–28

Day 1

1. Each new lesson will give you the opportunity to look back at the previous lesson in order to connect each to the other. What practical insights did you gain from the last discussion or lecture?

2. Why would James be concerned that too many in the community might take on the role of teaching (3:1-5a)?

3. In contrast to the damage James says the tongue can cause (3:2-5), what is something both positive and truthful you could say about someone else today (or during the week ahead)? (See Prov 10:21; 15:2, 4.)

Day 2

4. James warns that none of us can completely tame our tongues (3:8). Can you think of an example of someone—perhaps yourself—who endeavored to repair the damage done by an untamed tongue?

5. Why does James suggest that cursing human beings in some way attacks God (3:9)? (See Gen 1:26-27; 1 John 4:20.)

6. Why do you think that wisdom would produce humility rather than pride or something else (3:13)?

Day 3

7. How does what James says about wisdom and the fruit of righteousness (3:17-18) compare with Paul's description of the fruit of the Spirit? (See Gal 5:22-23.)

8. Many today claim that it is religious fanaticism that is the source of most conflicts in the world. What evidence do you see to validate James's claim that conflicts grow out of seeking to satisfy unbridled passions (4:1-2)?

9. If we are to receive what we pray for, how does James suggest we ought to change the way we pray (4:3-6)? (See Matt 21:22; Mark 11:24; Luke 11:9; John 16:24.)

Day 4

10. The heart of James's letter is said to be in his calling "adulterers" those who become enemies of God because of their love of the world (4:4). What might this have to do with his warnings against double mindedness (4:8; 1:8)? (See Matt 6:24; Luke 16:13; commentary, p. 23.)

11. What does Jesus say about passing judgment on others (4:11)? (See Matt 7:1-5; Luke 6:37.)

12. If James is not simply condemning those who make business plans, what is he suggesting for those who do business in the world (4:13-17)?

Day 5

13. How does what James says about the woes awaiting the rich (5:1-6) compare with what Jesus says about gathering treasure and also to Jesus' parable of Lazarus and the rich man? (See Matt 6:19-21; Luke 16:19-31.)

14. What examples of hardship and patience (5:10) are seen in the lives of Elijah and Jeremiah? (See 1 Kgs 19:1-8; Jer 38:1-6.)

15. What does Jesus say concerning those who persevere (5:11)? (See Matt 5:11-12.)

Day 6

16. As a society, how might we all benefit if our "Yes" meant "Yes" and our "No" meant "No" (5:12)? (See Matt 5:33-37.)

17. How does the church extend the ministry of Christ to those who suffer illness (5:13-15)? (See Mark 6:13.)

18. What experiences of answered prayer (5:16b) can you recount?

I Peter I:I–3:7

NCBC-NT VOLUME 10, PAGES 29–41

Day I

1. What is an example you can recall from James's letter that suggests he was familiar with at least some of the traditions of what Jesus had said and taught?

2. Peter's first letter is addressed "to the chosen sojourners of the dispersion" (1:1). Who does the commentary suggest these people are and how do they differ from the people addressed by James? (See commentary, pp. 30–33.)

3. How are the Father, the Spirit, and Jesus Christ each invoked at the beginning of this letter (1:2)?

Day 2

4. When Peter says the recipients of this letter may have to endure suffering "for a little while," what purpose does he suggest that suffering might achieve (1:6-7)? (See Matt 10:22; Acts 14:22; Rom 5:3-5.)

5. If, like the first readers of this letter, you believe in Christ and love him, even though you have not seen him, what most nurtures your faith and love (1:8-9)? (See John 20:29; 1 Cor 9:1; 1 John 1:1.)

6. Peter stresses both the freshness of the faith (1:8-9) and its antiquity (1:10-12). Why are both aspects important?

Day 3

7. What are some of the gifts or values dear to you that you have received because others chose to serve your needs rather than their own (1:12)?

8. Is personal awareness of being "born anew" something that belongs only to certain Protestants, or can Catholics lay claim to it as well (1:23)? (See John 3:1-8; 2 Cor 5:17; Titus 3:4-7; 1 Pet 1:23.)

9. Why are we to find reassurance in the quote from Isaiah that says we are like grass that withers (1:23-25)? (See Isa 40:6-8.)

Day 4

10. Peter says that, together, we are a holy priesthood, called to offer spiritual sacrifices (2:5). In your mind, what might some of these spiritual sacrifices be? (See Ps 50:14, 23; Heb 13:15.)

11. How can awareness of our own stumbling and disobedience make us more effective evangelizers (2:8)?

12. When you think of being "a people" (2:10), who are the different groups of "people" you feel yourself part of? Which are most important to you?

Day 5

13. a) What are some Christian values that, if practiced by all who profess to hold them, would win respect for the faith among people in general (2:12)?

    b) What are some of the admirable traits you recognize in non-Catholics and/or non-Christians in your civic community?

14. What questions of conscience might have arisen for some early Christians when told to "be subject to every human institution" (2:13)?

15. When might being faithful to Christ today commit one to resisting authorities or practicing "civil disobedience"? (See Matt 22:17-21; Acts 4:13-19; 5:27-29.)

Day 6

16. What were "household codes" and how did they influence the message of First Peter, especially 2:18–3:7? (See commentary, p. 39.)

17. a) To what ultimate purpose were slaves being asked to be subject to their masters (2:18-25)?

    b) How does Catholic teaching today provide a very different perspective on the whole matter of master-and-slave relationships?

18. Men and women are "joint heirs of the gift of life" (3:1-7). In what ways is this belief reflected in the changing roles of men and women today? (See Gal 3:27-28.)

I Peter 3:8–5:14

NCBC-NT VOLUME 10, PAGES 41–47

Day I

1. What do you consider the most memorable aspect of First Peter from last week's lesson?

2. If you can remember being insulted or treated poorly by someone, is it possible for you to pray a blessing for them now (3:8-9)? (See Luke 6:28; Rom 12:14.)

3. How can your own faith community be part of peacemaking efforts both locally and on a larger scale (3:10-11)? (See Matt 5:9.)

Day 2

4. What reasons can you give for the hope you have in Christ (3:15-16)?

5. Why is suffering for doing good better than suffering for having done wrong (3:17-18)? (See Rom 8:16-17; 2 Cor 1:5-7; Jas 1:2-3.)

6. Who might the "spirits in prison" be to whom Christ is said to have preached (3:19-20)? (See Gen 6:1-6.)

Day 3

7. What likeness does Peter see between the floodwaters of Noah's time and the water of baptism (3:19-22)? (See Gen 6–9; Rom 6:3-4; 1 Cor 10:1-2; Gal 3:27.)

8. If Christians today determined not to engage in any of the activities Peter lists as belonging to "Gentiles," in what ways might we expect to suffer as a result (4:1-3)? (See Rom 1:28-32.)

9. Why might early Christians have been particularly concerned about those faithful who had died (4:6)? (See 1 Thess 4:13-18; commentary, p. 44.)

Day 4

10. a) In what liturgical season are we most frequently reminded of the message "the end of all things is at hand" (4:7)?

    b) Why do you think that message is an important part of the Gospel? (See Matt 24:36-44; Mark 13:32-37; Luke 21:25-28; Acts 1:11; Rev 22:10-13.)

11. What gifts have you been given in order that you might serve others (4:10)? (See Rom 12:6-8; 1 Cor 12:4-10.)

12. a) Where are Christians today enduring a "trial by fire" (4:12)?

    b) Are there any instances today in your locales where certain religious beliefs are met with intolerance?

Day 5

13. How can individual Christians and local churches try to overcome the scandal created by those who have done evil while claiming association with Christ (4:14-18)?

14. What is a "presbyter" and what meaning did it have at the time First Peter was written (5:1-4)? (See Acts 14:23; 20:17; 1 Tim 4:14; 5:17; Titus 1:5; commentary, 45–46.)

15. What "shepherds" can you name who exemplify the virtuous leadership urged by Peter (5:1-4)? (See Matt 20:25-28; 1 Tim 3:1-14; Jas 3:1.)

Day 6

16. Why are Silvanus (also known as Silas) and Mark considered important figures in the early church (5:1-13)? (For Silas/Silvanus, see Acts 15:22, 27, 32, 40; 16:19, 25, 29; 17:4, 10, 14, 15; 18:5; 2 Cor 1:19; 1 Thess 1:1; 2 Thess 1:1; for Mark, see Acts 12:12, 25; 15:37, 39; Col 4:10; 2 Tim 4:11; Phlm 1:24.)

17. We are told this letter was probably written from Rome; what reasons might Peter have had for suggesting he was writing from Babylon (5:13)? (See Rev 14:8; 17:5; 18:2; commentary, pp. 29, 47.)

18. How have we incorporated greeting one another "with a loving kiss" into our liturgy (5:14)? (See Rom 16:16; 1 Cor 16:20; 2 Cor 13:12; 1 Thess 5:26.)

2 Peter 1:1–2:16; Jude vv. 1-13

NCBC-NT VOLUME 10, PAGES 48–54; 57–67

All Scripture references noted in parenthesis are to 2 Peter unless otherwise indicated.

Day 1

1. As you move on to study another letter in the New Testament, what do you hope most to remember from your study of First Peter?

2. The commentary tells us that the literary style of Second Peter is that of a *testament*. What are some of the characteristics of a testament found in Second Peter? (See commentary, p. 59.)

3. Why are both Second Peter and Jude considered one of the New Testament's "catholic" letters (1:1; Jude v. 1)? (See commentary, p. 58.)

Day 2

4. Though they use different words, how do both Second Peter and Jude emphasize the unity in the faith they share with their letters' recipients (1:1; Jude v. 3)? (See 2 Pet 3:1; 1 Pet 1:1.)

5. What do Peter and Jude pray those who read their letters might have in abundance (1:2; Jude v. 2)?

6. a) What does Peter say is the goal of the promises God has bestowed on us (1:3-4)? (See Rom 6:5; 1 John 3:2.)

   b) What does that mean to you?

Day 3

7. Peter urges his readers to supplement their faith with a number of virtues (2:5-7). How might one go about doing this?

8. What does Peter's reference to his body as a "tent" suggest about all our lives here on earth (1:12)? (See Deut 26:5; 1 Cor 4:11-12a; 2 Cor 5:1-4.)

9. Considering what the commentary says about the authorship of Second Peter, how might the letter itself be an example of Peter's promise to "make every effort to enable you always to remember these things after my departure" (1:15)? (See commentary, pp. 57–58.)

Day 4

10. a) What event is Peter referring to when he writes of being an eyewitness to Jesus' glory (1:16-18)? (See Mark 9:2-9.)

    b) Who else were witnesses of this event? (See Matt 17:1-9; Luke 9:28-36.)

    c) Does the letter of Jude refer to this event?

11. Since interpretation of prophecy (and all of Scripture) is not a matter to be trusted solely to private interpretation (1:21), how does one safely grow in knowledge and understanding of the Bible? (See Matt 13:52; Luke 24:44-45; 2 Tim 3:16.)

12. Peter warns against the likely danger of false teachers (2:1-3). Who (and what) have been the reliable sources in your growth in understanding of the faith?

Day 5

13. Peter assures us that the Lord knows how to rescue the devout even as evil is punished (2:9). What examples does he give of this (2:4-9)? (See Gen 6:1–8:22; 19:1-26.)

14. Almost everything written in the letter of Jude reappears in Second Peter. What reason does the commentary suggest for Second Peter leaving out Jude's references to the archangel Michael and the body of Moses (Jude v. 9)? (See commentary, p. 57.)

15. Jude and Peter both concern themselves with those who revile angels and "glorious beings" (2:10; Jude v. 8). In what way, if any, do angels play a role in your faith life? (See Matt 18:10; Luke 15:10; Col 2:18.)

Day 6

16. What does Jude suggest as an alternative to "a reviling judgment" when confronting forces or powers beyond our understanding (vv. 8-13, see v. 9 in particular)? (See Matt 7:1-2.)

17. What are the "love feasts" Jude refers to (v. 12.)? (See 1 Cor 11:17-34.)

18. What is the Old Testament account of Balaam (2:15-16)? (See Num 22:4–24:25; 31:8; Deut 23:4-6; Josh 13:21b-22.)

2 Peter 2:17–3:18; Jude vv. 14-24

NCBC-NT VOLUME 10, PAGES 54–56; 66–71

All Scripture references noted in parenthesis are to 2 Peter unless otherwise indicated.

Day 1

1. What is something significant to you that you can recall from last week's study of the first half of Second Peter and Jude?

2. Second Peter describes false teachers as waterless springs and gale-driven mists (2:17). What images from nature would you associate with those who *faithfully* teach the Gospel? (Use your imagination. See Isa 52:7; Matt 5:13, 14; 1 Pet 2:2.)

3. a) What ministries or social services are available in your community to help people overcome addictions (2:19)?

   b) Are there any of these services connected in any way to the ministries of your parish or diocese?

Day 2

4. Second Peter is very concerned about those who, having once believed, turn away from the faith (2:20-22). What programs or services are you aware of that attempt to bring nonpracticing Catholics back into full participation?

5. In ancient times, disciples considered it proper to give credit to their teachers as the true author of their writings. How might this explain what is claimed for Second Peter in 3:1?

6. Christians firmly believe that God, in Christ, has decisively acted in human history (3:1-7). Can you identify moments or aspects of your own life in which God has played an important role?

Day 3

7. a) How does Second Peter depict the culmination of world history (3:7)?

   b) How does Paul's understanding of the same culmination provide a different perspective of "the end"? (See Rom 8:18-21.)

8. a) How patient has God been with you (3:9)? (See Heb 5:2.)

   b) How important in your life has the need or desire been to learn the virtue of patience (3:9)? (See Prov 14:29; 15:18; 16:32; 1 Cor 13:4; Gal 5:22-23; 1 Thess 5:14.)

9. How is the theme of new heavens and a new earth (3:13) introduced in Isaiah and built lavishly upon in the book of Revelation? (See Isa 65:17-19; Rev 21.)

Day 4

10. Given the judgment Peter warns lies ahead (3:10-13), how is it possible to stand before God in peace (3:14)? (See Rom 5:1-2; 15:13; Heb 10:22; 1 Pet 3:21; 1 John 4:17-18.)

11. What do we read in Paul concerning the Lord's patience, or forbearance (3:15)? (See Rom 2:4; 3:21-26.)

12. If you agree with Peter that there are things Paul writes that are hard to understand, what are one or two of them that you can think of (3:16)?

Day 5

13. What does the commentary say is the significance of Second Peter inferring that Paul's letters are "scripture" (3:16)? (See commentary, pp. 58, 70.)

14. What does Genesis say about Enoch that led to him being an important figure, not only in Jude, but in other, nonscriptural writings (Jude vv. 14-15)? (See Gen 5:19-24.)

15. Jude warns that those who cause division are "devoid of the Spirit" (v. 19). What does Paul tell us characterizes those in whom the Spirit dwells? (See Rom 14:17; Gal 5:22-23.)

Day 6

16. What traditional spiritual works of mercy does Jude appear to be advocating in verses 22-23? (See Matt 18:15; Gal 6:1; Jas 5:19-20.)

17. What is something you hope to take with you in the days ahead that you have gathered from your study of these catholic letters of James, Peter, and Jude?

18. Both Jude and Second Peter end with a doxology, that is, a hymn of praise. You are encouraged to do the same at the conclusion of this study by reciting aloud the "Glory Be" or some other act of praise. (Glory be to the Father, and to the Son, and to the Holy Spirit, as it was in the beginning, is now, and will be forever. Amen.)

ABBREVIATIONS

Books of the Bible

Gen—Genesis
Exod—Exodus
Lev—Leviticus
Num—Numbers
Deut—Deuteronomy
Josh—Joshua
Judg—Judges
Ruth—Ruth
1 Sam—1 Samuel
2 Sam—2 Samuel
1 Kgs—1 Kings
2 Kgs—2 Kings
1 Chr—1 Chronicles
2 Chr—2 Chronicles
Ezra—Ezra
Neh—Nehemiah
Tob—Tobit
Jdt—Judith
Esth—Esther
1 Macc—1 Maccabees
2 Macc—2 Maccabees
Job—Job
Ps(s)—Psalm(s)
Prov—Proverbs
Eccl—Ecclesiastes
Song—Song of Songs
Wis—Wisdom
Sir—Sirach
Isa—Isaiah
Jer—Jeremiah
Lam—Lamentations
Bar—Baruch
Ezek—Ezekiel
Dan—Daniel
Hos—Hosea
Joel—Joel
Amos—Amos

Obad—Obadiah
Jonah—Jonah
Mic—Micah
Nah—Nahum
Hab—Habakkuk
Zeph—Zephaniah
Hag—Haggai
Zech—Zechariah
Mal—Malachi
Matt—Matthew
Mark—Mark
Luke—Luke
John—John
Acts—Acts
Rom—Romans
1 Cor—1 Corinthians
2 Cor—2 Corinthians
Gal—Galatians
Eph—Ephesians
Phil—Philippians
Col—Colossians
1 Thess—1 Thessalonians
2 Thess—2 Thessalonians
1 Tim—1 Timothy
2 Tim—2 Timothy
Titus—Titus
Phlm—Philemon
Heb—Hebrews
Jas—James
1 Pet—1 Peter
2 Pet—2 Peter
1 John—1 John
2 John—2 John
3 John—3 John
Jude—Jude
Rev—Revelation